Bad Memories

Getting Past Your Past

Resources for Changing Lives

A Ministry of
THE CHRISTIAN COUNSELING AND
EDUCATIONAL FOUNDATION
Glenside, Pennsylvania

RCL Ministry Booklets
Susan Lutz, Series Editor

Bad Memories

Getting Past Your Past

Robert D. Jones

P&R
PUBLISHING
P.O. BOX 817 • PHILLIPSBURG • NEW JERSEY 08865-0817

© 2004 by Robert D. Jones

Printed in the United States of America

Library of Congress Cataloging-in-Publication Data

Jones, Robert D., 1959–
    Bad memories : getting past your past / Robert D. Jones.
        p.   cm. — (Resources for changing lives)
    Includes bibliographical references.
    ISBN 10: 0-87552-661-6
    ISBN 13: 978-0-87552-661-4
    1. Memory—Religious aspects—Christianity.
2. Forgiveness of sin. I. Title. II. Series.

BV4597.565J66 2004
234'.5—dc22   2004049542

Besieged with dark memories, Holly did little more each day than cope. Her past sexual sins and attempted suicide troubled her daily. Ever since he'd learned of these things shortly after their marriage, her husband Jim had tried to be supportive. But the fact that she had hidden her sins from Jim only increased Holly's feelings of guilt. Day and night a depressive cloud hung over her as she recalled her past. The fact that she had committed these sins as a Christian only doubled her misery. She *had* known better, and now she hated her life.

Todd too was troubled by his past. His failing hardware business brought mounting debts, and his get-rich schemes yielded little more than financial misery for him and his wife. Angry tantrums became nightly events. His increased drinking and growing rage only distanced him from Janet and the kids, resulting finally in a bitter divorce. "Why did I say those things about her in front of the children? I knew they weren't true," he later admitted to his pastor. "I'm the one who ruined our marriage, not her. And there's nothing I can do about it now."

Is there help and hope in Christ for Holly and Todd, and for others who suffer because of their own past? Do the memories of your past haunt you? Perhaps it was one big sin, or maybe some chronic pattern of wrong behavior. The memories can plague and cripple you.

If you struggle with your past, you are not alone. Listen to this assessment by a wise pastor, D. Martyn Lloyd-Jones:

> The problem here is the case of those who are miserable or who are suffering from spiritual depression because of their past—either because of some particular sin in their past, or because of the particular form which sin happened to take in their case. I would say that in my experience in the ministry extending now over many years, there is no more common difficulty. It is constantly recurring and I think that I have had to deal with more people over this particular thing than over anything else.[1]

God in his Word provides a solution to this haunting problem, a powerful and life-changing solution beyond any we could imagine. What is God's answer?

Our Goal Is Memory Transformation

Let's begin by defining our goal. Most people who suffer from bad memories simply want them to disappear. They tell me, "I just want to forget the past. I wish it would all go away." What they want, simply put, is memory erasure.

If eradicating the past is your goal, the world offers a menu of escapes. You can dull your memories by drug or alcohol abuse. "I drank to forget the pain," Todd later confessed. Holly settled for a combination of therapeutic "memory healing" and prescription tranquilizers. Some beleaguered people opt for electroconvulsive shock treatments or demon deliverance ministries. What they all have in common is a rid-the-memory agenda.

On the other hand, some would-be helpers seem to deny the problem and urge a different goal, a just-forget-the-past agenda. Some Christians appeal to Philippians 3:13 ("forgetting those things which are behind"), urging people plagued by bad memories to "just put it behind you and get on with your life." That was the counsel Holly received from a radio preacher. "When bad thoughts come, just pray and press on with reading your Bible, going to church, and serving Jesus. Don't dwell on the past; live for the present."

While this sounds attractive, this agenda is misleading and insensitive to suffering people. For one thing, it misinterprets Philippians 3:13. Paul is not talking about forgetting his past sins. He is talking about the way he once tried to get right with God through his religious achievement instead of through Jesus. Paul does not tell people to "just forget about your past thievery." Moreover, the counsel is pastorally unkind. It's true that prayer, Scripture, church, and Christian service are vital parts of God's answer, but the "just-forget-the-past" approach does not place those rich disciplines in their gospel context. Without the gospel, these disciplines offer little help to people who can't shut off the bad memory flow. Further, this agenda settles for too little. It misses God's greater goal for us: Christ-likeness.

The good news, however, is that if you belong to Jesus, God *does* have something better for you. God does not want to *remove* your memories; he wants to *redeem* them. He wants to *transform* them into something good, something that will make you more like Jesus.

Do you see the hope this offers Christians? Your bad memories of your past sins—even the worst ones—can be opportunities for life-changing growth. You do not need to avoid, run from, cover over, or get rid of your past. You can reinterpret it God's way. God's goal is neither memory erasure nor memory denial, but memory redemption.

A Biblical Perspective on Memories

How can God redeem your recurring memories of past failures? By giving you his perspective on them. A gospel-centered perspective of faith and hope will help you to realize three things.

1. God was in your past. He was not asleep or on vacation when you did or said the evil things that now trouble you. Whether you committed those sins before or after you became a Christian, the sovereign God was on site. He now intends to turn your past into something good. This is the perspective Joseph models in Genesis 50:20, when he reflected on his brothers' treacherous sins: "You intended to harm me, but God intended it for good." (See also Gen. 45:5–7; Acts 17:25–31; Rom. 8:28–29; Eph. 1:4, 11; and Jer. 29:11.)

2. Your past does not control your future. Your past might *influence* your present beliefs or actions, but you are not a hostage to what you did or what happened to you. You are not doomed. Instead, you are a new creation in Christ (2 Cor. 5:17), forgiven and set free. In that context you are a responsible human being, and an active interpreter and responder to your situation. You are fully accountable for your present choices no matter what memories linger (see Gen. 37–50; Prov. 4:23; Mark 7:14–23; and James 1:13–15). The question is, will you trust God's forgiveness and his ability to use evil for good? Will you reflect this in the choices and responses you make?

3. Your memories result from your *interpretation* of your past (see Gen. 50:20; Rom. 8:28–29; Num. 11; Ps. 78:11, 106:13; and Ezek. 16). What you actually remember are not the past events *per se*, but the past-events-as-you-interpret-them. They are not "bare" facts, but interpreted facts. This means that they are capable of *re*interpretation. That is where your hope lies. The hope of the gospel can help you put the right interpretation on your past and make it into a good thing for you. This is what will help you get past your past!

Soon after moving to West Virginia, I lost

my eyeglasses. Being lazy, cheap, and too proud to admit visual decline, I went several years without replacing them. Eventually, after an eye exam and some loving pressure from my wife, I broke down and bought a new pair. I instantly entered a new world. Billboards suddenly became legible. Little items enlarged. Colors brightened. Contrasts cleared. The glasses had corrected my vision and allowed me to see things the way they really are.

The same is true of your memories. As you put on the Bible's glasses to gain a Christ-centered perspective, you see your past differently. Like Joseph, you can draw positive conclusions about God's all-powerful, all-wise, and all-loving purposes for *all* of your life.

Three Marks of a Redeemed Memory

The question is: How should we interpret our past sins so that God's redemptive purposes can be realized in our lives? The apostle Paul's real-life example can direct us. Near the end of his ministry, Paul writes to Timothy to fortify his fearful young friend with God's strength. In 1 Timothy 1:12–17, Paul recalls his own call to ministry, which came to him while he actively persecuted the church of Jesus. Listen to his testimony:

I thank Christ Jesus our Lord, who has given me strength, that he considered me faithful, appointing me to his service. Even though I was once a blasphemer and a persecutor and a violent man, I was shown mercy because I acted in ignorance and unbelief. The grace of our Lord was poured out on me abundantly, along with the faith and love that are in Christ Jesus. Here is a trustworthy saying that deserves full acceptance: Christ Jesus came into the world to save sinners—of whom I am the worst. But for that very reason I was shown mercy so that in me, the worst of sinners, Christ Jesus might display his unlimited patience as an example for those who would believe on him and receive eternal life. Now to the King eternal, immortal, invisible, the only God, be honor and glory forever and ever. Amen.

Paul doesn't hide his sinful past; instead, he presents a gospel interpretation of it. He doesn't flee, avoid, or forget his past; he looks at it through God's lens. This is why the passage ends on a positive note. Jesus saves and transforms even big sinners like Paul, and God is exalted in the process. When Paul views his past through a Christ-centered, gospel lens, his life is characterized by a deepening repentance, heightened gratitude, and broader effectiveness in helping others. Let's examine each element in turn.

Deepening Repentance

Honestly facing the ugliness of your past failures deepens your repentance. In the verses above, Paul recalls how evil he was. He blasphemed God, a capital offense for a Jew. In his anti-Christian zeal, he persecuted Christ's church. He was a violent man, overseeing the beating and stoning of disciples like Stephen in Acts 7. Yet Paul does not avoid recalling these sins or try to forget them. Instead, he reminds himself, and Timothy, of his wickedness.

What is the value of being conscious of your past sins? For one thing, it will drive you to seek reconciliation and restitution with those you have mistreated (if you have not already done so). Perhaps certain sins hound you simply because they are unresolved. Nagging thoughts about past sins might signal a need to reconcile a relationship. Further work might be needed.

Sandra's relationship with her mother demonstrated this. For twenty years, Sandra wrestled with guilt daily about mistreating her mom. It had begun when she rudely rejected her mother's sensible counsel about college, career, and marriage choices. Later attempts to rebuild the relationship failed, and Sandra's guilt compounded. "I can't believe how hardheaded I was back then," she sadly admits. Only when Sandra repented and sought her mother's forgiveness did her struggle resolve. The bad memories in turn have slowly faded.

Being conscious of your sins will also sensitize you to new temptations in the same areas. Like a child once burned by a stove, you will be more careful next time, quicker to watch and pray about this area of weakness. Remembering your past evil will deter you from repeating it. "As a dog returns to its vomit, so a fool repeats his folly" (Prov. 26:11). The repentant, former adulterer will avoid the first step that led him down that destructive path.

In Romans 6, Paul expands on this dynamic, reminding us of God's grace in Christ. Union with the crucified, risen Christ grants us a clean record and a brand new life. Yet, even in the course of this gospel encouragement, Paul recalls our past sin: "What benefit did you reap at that time from the things you are now ashamed of? Those things result in death!" (Rom. 6:21).

Why does Paul stir up our memories of past sins? Isn't that counter-productive? Bible scholar Leon Morris observes, "We should not miss the force of his *now*. While they were the slaves of sin they were not ashamed. . . . To be without shame is a mark of a sin-dominated life. But when they became Christians they came to see sin for the evil thing it is and their past deeds for the shameful things they were."[2] John Calvin contends from this verse that only those "who have learned well to be earnestly dissatisfied with themselves, and to be confounded with shame at their wretchedness" truly understand the Christian gospel.[3]

Yet someone objects, "It's not right for Christians to feel such shame. Shame is bad." Contemporary psychologies (even some "Christian" versions) agree. But that simplistic conclusion misses the depths of God's Word. Of course, believers in Jesus must be convinced that in Christ there is no condemnation (Rom. 8:1). We must bask daily in the sunlight of God's love. We must trust in his cleansing forgiveness and drink the living water he offers.

Yet the same Bible also describes a legitimate sense of lingering shame that we *should* have about our past sins. Like the apostle Paul, the prophet Ezekiel viewed this kind of shame as good fruit: the godly fruit of repentance in response to God's grace promised in the new covenant. Ezekiel 16 promises, "However, I will restore . . . your fortunes along with them, so that you may bear your disgrace and be ashamed of all you have done in giving them comfort" (16:53–54). Commenting on this text, John Taylor recalls some famous examples: "Paul remembered that he had persecuted the church (1 Cor. 15:9; 1 Tim. 1:13); John Newton remembered his slave-trading days. The value of such memory is that it keeps a man back from pride. Not even the justified sinner should forget that he has a past of which he is right to be ashamed."[4] There is no contradiction between a present enjoyment of justification and a proper sense of shame about past sin. Both mark the maturing Christian.

Ezekiel continues, "Yet I will remember the covenant I made with you in the days of your youth, and I will establish an everlasting covenant with you. Then you will remember your ways and be ashamed. . . . Then, when I make atonement for you for all you have done, you will remember and be ashamed" (Ezek.

16:60–63). Again, Taylor observes, "Israel's reaction will be that she will be shamed by God's goodness into a state of repentance and self-loathing (*cf.* Ezek. 20:43), and will therefore acknowledge God in a way that she has failed to before."[5] The fruit of grace includes a godly form of self-loathing.

Or consider the famous new heart/new covenant promise in Ezekiel 36:22–32. God promises to save, cleanse, and bless his people. The result? "Then you will remember your evil ways and wicked deeds, and you will loathe yourselves for your sins and detestable practices. I want you to know that I am not doing this for your sake, declares the Sovereign LORD. Be ashamed and disgraced for your conduct, O house of Israel!" (Ezek. 36:31–32). Far from being a bad thing, godly shame is affirmed.

What do the apostle Paul and the prophet Ezekiel teach us? Properly remembering our past sins with shame will deter us from repeating them and help us receive God's saving grace. When we recall our failures through the lens of Christ's mercy, God produces in us ongoing repentance and deepening humility.

Years ago, a woman I was counseling came to a small group meeting I was to lead. Mary's counseling growth assignments included a prayer journal of her progress in fighting the problem we identified. Before the group started, she privately slipped me a copy of her journal so that I could read it before our counseling the next day. Mary then innocently asked me what we were going to do in the group that night. I looked at her and with a straight face replied, "I thought we would read and discuss your journal with the group."

To this day I shudder with shame. Though I never intended to share her journal with the group, my sick "joke" displayed inexcusable pastoral insensitivity. You might imagine Mary's hurt. To violate her trust and to treat so flippantly the fine china of her private journal was a grievous offense. "Reckless words pierce like a sword," says Proverbs 12:18, and I had gashed this Christian sister.

God helped me to quickly repent and to seek (and receive) her forgiveness, but the shameful memory lives on, even though God has redeemed it. To paraphrase Genesis 50:20, I meant it for evil, but God meant it for good! From this perspective, I gladly thank God for the lessons my memory brings. It reminds me that, apart from Jesus, I am a hard-core sinner.

It tells me that being a biblical counselor does not immunize me from the dangers of insensitivity. It teaches me to treat strugglers with care, and to guard the delicate life data they confide to me.

What do you do when sinful memories swarm into your mind? Acknowledge before God their sinfulness, without excuse. Thank him for another reminder of the sinfulness of sin. And renew your commitment, with the Spirit's help, to put that sin to death and to replace it with Christ-like thinking and behavior.

Heightened Gratitude

The second way our sinful memories are redeemed is seen when we let them heighten our gratitude to God for his mercy to us in Christ.

Returning to Paul's example in 1 Timothy 1:12–17, we find that he not only recalls his past sin, but he also praises God for his grace. And he does both, at the same time, in the very same passage. "I thank Christ Jesus our Lord" (v. 12). "Even though I was once a blasphemer and a persecutor and a violent man, I was shown mercy. . . ." (v. 13). In the same breath, Paul recalls his terrible sins *and* gives thanks to Jesus! There is no contradiction here. Viewed rightly (that is, redemptively), our evil magnifies God's mercy. "The grace of our Lord was poured out on me abundantly, along with the faith and love that are in Christ Jesus" (v. 14).

Listen to his "trustworthy statement" in verses 15–16: "Christ Jesus came into the world to save sinners—of whom I am the worst. . . . I was shown mercy." Paul ends in a majestic doxology, "Now to the King eternal, immortal, invisible, the only God, be honor and glory for ever and ever. Amen" (v. 17).

Paul's balance is brilliant. On the one hand, he does not forget or avoid his past. He freely admits he was a blasphemer, a persecutor, and a violent man. On the other hand, he does not dwell on these facts. He dwells on Jesus' saving work and on God's mercy in sending such a Savior. Paul lets his past highlight God's grace. The sinner that Jesus came to save is a real sinner with a shameful past.

Paul is not the only sinner in Scripture. In Luke 7:36–50, Jesus visits the home of Simon the Pharisee. A notoriously sinful woman enters, boldly washes Jesus' feet with her tears and hair, and kisses and anoints his feet with perfume. Simon protests: Jesus must not allow such a "sinner" to defile him. Jesus responds with a simple parable: " 'Two men owed money to a certain moneylender. One owed him five hundred denarii, and the other fifty. Neither of them had the money to pay him back, so he canceled the debts of both. Now which of them will love him more?' Simon replied, 'I suppose the one who had the bigger debt canceled.' 'You have judged correctly,' Jesus said" (vv. 41–43).

Jesus applies the illustration by rebuking self-righteous Simon and commending the sinful woman (vv. 44–46). He reinforces our main point: "Therefore, I tell you, her many sins have been forgiven—for she loved much. But he who has been forgiven little loves little" (v. 47).

What motivates this woman's deep love for Jesus? His forgiveness of her many sins! The Lord teaches that those who have been forgiven much (like her) love much, while those who view Jesus' mercy as a little thing (like Simon) will show him little love.

In other words, big sinners need a big Savior, and they respond with big praise!

When we let our past memories springboard us to higher views of God's grace, it energizes our praise and solidifies our Christian confidence. Few texts are more comforting than 1 Timothy 1:15, "Christ Jesus came into the world to save sinners—of whom I am the worst." Can you feel Paul's joy as he recounts the work of Jesus?

As shameful as our sins may be, we must never fixate on them. The Scottish minister Robert Murray M'Cheyne used to say, "For every one look at your sin, take ten looks at Jesus Christ." We must focus on Jesus, the Savior who fully and forever forgives our sins and cleanses us from all unrighteousness. In him, we find mercy and help, and we can convert our bad memories into beneficial ones.

In his book, *The Cross Centered Life*, Pastor C. J. Mahaney echoes this truth from his own life. In his high school and college years he was immersed in the drug culture and rebellious toward God. Then God saved him. Now, living in the same locale, C. J. regularly faces reminders of his past. Tragic, you say? Hardly. Listen to his testimony:

> Many people today try to run from the past. I suppose I could try to as well, by leaving the hometown that holds so many reminders of my sinfulness. But I consider living here a gift from God. The regular reminders of my past are precious to me. Why? Because, like

Paul, I never want to forget the great
mercy shown to me.[6]

How can past sinful memories be a *gift* from
God? What can make them *precious*? The
transforming grace of God. "I never want to
forget the great mercy shown to me."

This means that when the dandelions of
your past spring up—unwelcome and unin-
vited—you must seize them as opportunities to
remember the cross. "Yes, Lord, I sinned, and I
am ashamed," you confess. "But Jesus paid for
my sin. He absorbed the wrath that I deserved.
I am now forgiven—fully forgiven—as far as
the east is from the west. Please weed these
memories from my mind. But until you do, I
will praise you for your saving grace in Jesus my
Lord."

One husband learned this only after his divorce and remarriage. He and his new wife came
to me for counseling. It soon became clear to all
of us that he had dragged the unresolved guilt of
his first marriage into his second one. Our counseling agenda shifted. He examined his sins
against his ex-wife, repented before God, and
chose to write her a confession letter. He admitted his failure, sought her forgiveness, and spoke
of God's grace. Then he added these words, "I

often think of my failures in our marriage. But this is helping me to learn to thank God for his forgiveness. I can't erase what I did, but I can let God use it to make me grateful for his grace." He was learning to let his past sin become a present occasion to exalt Christ's mercy.[7]

This truth is not limited to the *forgiving* grace of God. Paul applied it to God's *empowering* grace in 1 Corinthians 15:9–10:

> For I am the least of the apostles and do not even deserve to be called an apostle, because I persecuted the church of God. But by the grace of God I am what I am, and his grace to me was not without effect. No, I worked harder than all of them—yet not I, but the grace of God that was with me.

Paul's recollection that his apostleship was undeserved highlights God's work in calling him and energizing him in this ministry.

We see in these passages what these truths do for individuals. Can you imagine what happens when a whole congregation grasps them? Worship soars and testimonies flow. May God fill us, his church, with a growing appreciation of his grace toward us!

Broader Effectiveness in Helping Others

Finally, when God helps you to reinterpret your past sins from a gospel perspective, your bad memories can broaden your effectiveness in ministering to others.

After describing himself in 1 Timothy 1:15 as the worst sinner, Paul declares in verse 16, "But for that very reason I was shown mercy so that in me, the worst of sinners, Christ Jesus might display his unlimited patience as an example for those who would believe on him and receive eternal life."

Why did Christ display his unlimited patience toward Paul? "As an example for those who would believe. . . ." Paul saw his life as a pattern for what God will do for others. God's forgiveness of *his* sins breeds hope for Paul's hearers. This theme became part of Paul's life message. In Timothy's case, Paul knew that this was part of the encouragement Timothy needed to confidently preach the gospel—to give hope to other sinners by using Paul's example.

What effect does this have on ministering to other sinners? For one thing, you can understand their problem experientially. You can relate to fellow failures. You know sin's shame. As a sinner, Paul has "been there," right alongside other serious sinners. Blessed by God, your sinful past can increase your sensitivity and compassion.

Furthermore, you can offer hope by holding out your life as an example of God's hope at work. Your wrongs did not end your life; neither must they end your friend's. You can lead him to Christ's answers. You can tell him how God forgave all your sins, and retrained your mind to reinterpret your memories.

Second Corinthians 1 demonstrates this perspective as Paul recalls God's work in his life, and the way it enables him to serve the Corinthians:

> Praise be to the God and Father of our Lord Jesus Christ, the Father of compassion and the God of all comfort, who comforts us in all our troubles, so that we can comfort those in any trouble with the comfort we ourselves have received from God. (2 Cor. 1:3–4)

God's comfort enables Paul to comfort others as well. While Paul does not mention his struggles with ugly memories here, he is acutely conscious of his tendencies toward sinful self-reliance:

> We do not want you to be uninformed, brothers, about the hardships we suffered in the province of Asia. We were under great pressure, far beyond our ability to endure, so that we despaired even of life. Indeed, in our hearts we felt the sentence of death. But this happened that we might not rely on ourselves but on God, who raises the dead. (2 Cor. 1:8–9)

Paul's experience of God's grace, amid his own sinful temptations, gave him confidence in ministering to the Corinthians. In verses 10–11 he anticipates the impact this deliverance would have on others.

Jason learned a painful lesson when adultery ended his career in Christian ministry. Churches in his denomination close the pastoral door to those who sin in these ways. "I know God has forgiven me, but I feel so defeated. How can God use me after what I've done?" Grasping Paul's perspective bred hope. Jason's sins did not end his ministry to people. Despair yielded to vision as he thought of others facing the same temptations. Along with deepening his repentance and heightening his appreciation of grace, God began to use him to help those who had sinned in similar ways, as well as those on temptation's edge. He and his wife have helped other couples walk down God's path of confession and forgiveness and rebuild their marriages. God redeemed Jason's trespasses and his redeemed memories now aid his ministry.

When reminders of your past invade, don't question your kingdom usefulness. That is Satan's ploy to derail you. Instead, thank God for his commitment to work through your folly to make you more sensitive to fellow sinners. Ask him to open doors of relational ministry and to give you the wisdom and courage, like the apostle Paul, to testify of his life-changing grace in your life.

Conclusion

You may not be able to prevent sinful memories from arising. Painful thoughts might still intrude without invitation. Yet you don't need to erase them or escape them. They do not have to destroy you. Birds of guilt may land on your head but they need not nest there. Your Redeemer is bigger than your past.

In Christ, your past can be redeemed. You

can learn to reinterpret it biblically. As 1 Timothy 1 teaches, a gospel-centered understanding of your past sin *deepens* your repentance, *heightens* your gratitude for God's saving grace, and *broadens* your effectiveness in helping others with wisdom and compassion.

May God redeem your nagging memories so that you might go deeper, higher, and broader, for his glory and your good.

Notes

1 D. Martyn Lloyd-Jones, *Spiritual Depression: Its Causes and Its Cure* (Grand Rapids: Eerdmans, 1965), p. 66.

2 Leon Morris, *The Epistle to the Romans* (Grand Rapids: Eerdmans, 1992), p. 266.

3 John Calvin, *The Epistles of Paul the Apostle to the Romans and Thessalonians*, trans. R. Mackenzie. In David W. Torrance and Thomas F. Torrance, eds., *Calvin's New Testament Commentaries*, (Grand Rapids: Eerdmans, 1979), 8:135.

4 John B. Taylor, *Ezekiel: An Introduction and Commentary*. In *Tyndale Old Testament Commentaries*, (Downers Grove, IL: Inter-Varsity Press, 1969), 20:142.

5 Ibid., p. 233.

6 C. J. Mahaney with Kevin Heath, *The Cross Centered Life* (Sisters, OR: Multnomah, 2002), p. 13.

7 For a thorough treatment of resolving past and present conflicts, I recommend Ken Sande, *The Peace-*

maker: *A Biblical Guide to Resolving Personal Conflict*, 3rd ed. (Grand Rapids: Baker, 2003); and Ken Sande with Tom Raabe, *Peacemaking for Families: A Biblical Guide to Managing Conflict in Your Home* (Wheaton, IL: Tyndale, 2002). The first resource is general; the second addresses marriage and family relationships.

Robert D. Jones *is associate professor of biblical counseling at Southeastern Baptist Theological Seminary.*

RCL Ministry Booklets

Pornography: Slaying the Dragon, by David Powlison

Pre-Engagement: 5 Questions to Ask Yourselves, by David Powlison and John Yenchko

Priorities: Mastering Time Management, by James C. Petty

Procrastination: First Steps to Change, by Walter Henegar

Self-Injury: When Pain Feels Good, by Edward T. Welch

Sexual Sin: Combatting the Drifting and Cheating, by Jeffrey S. Black

Stress: Peace amid Pressure, by David Powlison

Suffering: Eternity Makes a Difference, by Paul David Tripp

Suicide: Understanding and Intervening, by Jeffrey S. Black

Teens and Sex: How Should We Teach Them? by Paul David Tripp

Thankfulness: Even When It Hurts, by Susan Lutz

Why Me?: Comfort for the Victimized, by David Powlison

Worry: Pursuing a Better Path to Peace, by David Powlison